How to Become a Millionaire: Mastering the Inner Game of Wealth

Easy Proven Methods to Rocket your Income to Next Level

by

Praveen Kumar & Prashant Kumar

Disclaimer

The advice contained in this material might not be suitable for everyone. The author obtained the information from sources believed to be reliable and from his own personal experience, but he neither implies nor intends any guarantee of accuracy.

The author, publisher and distributors never give legal, accounting, medical or any other type of professional advice. The reader must always seek those services from competent professionals that can review their own particular circumstances.

The author, publisher and distributors particularly disclaim any liability, loss, or risk taken by individuals who directly or indirectly act on the information contained herein. All readers must accept full responsibility for their use of this material.

All pictures used in this book are for illustrative purposes only. The people in the pictures are not connected with the book, author or publisher and no link or endorsement between any of them and the topic or content is implied, nor should any be assumed. The pictures are only licensed for use in this book and must not be used for any other

Table of contents

INTRODUCTION 7

LIMITING BELIEFS THAT HOLD US BACK 15

HOW TO CHANGE YOUR ATTITUDE.................................25

TRIGGERS THAT WORK THE MIND 35

HOW TO OVERCOME FEAR? 45

GETTING OUT OF THE COMFORT ZONE 69

HOW TO RE-WIRE TO BECOME AN ENLIGHTENED MILLIONAIRE 75

DRIVING FORCE BEHIND WEALTH CREATION........... 115

OTHER BOOKS BY THE AUTHOR 121

ABOUT THE AUTHORS... 123

Introduction

Have you ever wondered what separates school dropouts, wealth creators like Bill Gates and Thomas Edison, from the highly educated professionals who rent their brains to the highest bidder?

Specialized knowledge is amongst the most plentiful and cheapest form of service which may be harnessed! If you doubt this, refer the payroll of any university. The difference lies in the mindset. If you think of jobs you will become an employee and help someone else become rich. If you think like a millionaire then you will become a millionaire. Once you acquire the mindset of a billionaire there is no force on earth that can stop you from becoming a billionaire.

This book is about inner engineering on how to reset your mind to becoming a wealth creator. It is designed to draw you out and develop you from within. It is about removing chaff from the wheat and going right into the heart and fundamentals of wealth creation as a process which will help you become an enlightened millionaire whether you are in business or an investor or aspire to be one.

The book reveals secrets of internal principles of wealth creation. Without understanding and incorporating the inner principles, it is not possible to apply the external principles of wealth creation in a sustainable way. Once you re-engineer your mindset, there is nothing stopping you from achieving your destiny of becoming truly wealthy.

There is no greater creativity or nobler cause than becoming an enlightened millionaire. The good news is that anyone can do it without exception, even if you don't have a dime in your pocket.

Once you understand the principles and acquire the right mindset of a wealth creator, you will be like a magnet attracting riches. Money will come to you so quickly and in such abundance that you will wonder as to where will wonder as to where it had been hiding during the lean years.

"If you want to change the fruits, you will first have to change the roots. If you want to change the visible, you must first change the invisible"

- T. Harv Eker

Every beautiful poem that was ever written, a great work of painting or sculpture that captivated you, a song or a book that captured your heart and mind, started as a simple thought in someone's mind. Just look around you – the bed you sleep in, the computer you work on, the shoes you walk in, the car you drive and the house you live in, or the stylish clothes you wear – everything was brought into existence with an idea that made money for its author.

It is the impulses of thought that have created air planes, space ships, skyscrapers and every invention you see on this planet. There was no nuclear power until someone visualized it. There was no radio or television until the time someone tapped onto radio waves. There was no electric bulb before Edison invented it.

Nietzsche rightly put it, *"Everyone thinks that the principal thing to the tree is the fruit, but in point of fact, the principal thing to it is the seed."* It is always the seed that precedes the tree and the fruits. We run after the fruits but the actual thing is the seed.

According to the Upanishads (ancient Hindu text that was written thousands of years ago,) even the universe was created when God had an idea. He said, *"I am one, let me be many."* The universe was thus created. This is supported by the Big Bang theory that the scientists have propounded of late; even they do not understand what caused the Big Bang! Is the world around us a manifestation of God's thought process? These are philosophical questions which all of us ponder when we search for answers. There is a lot of merit in this argument.

Thoughts are indeed the most powerful instrument of creation. Napoleon Hill, in his book *Think and Grow Rich* writes, "***Truly, "thoughts are things" and powerful at that, when they are mixed with definite of purpose, persistence, and a burning desire for translation into riches, or other material objects. All earned riches have their beginning in an idea.***"

If you want to have a bite of the 'rich fruit,' then you have first to change the roots that nourish the tree and the fruit; what is visible is just a manifestation of what is not visible. Your wealth is the extension of your thought process. If you have the mindset of a millionaire, you will become a millionaire. Once you expand your mental state to be that of a billionaire, then there is nothing on earth that will stop you from becoming a billionaire.

There is no doubt that starting point of all riches is in the seeding-the thought process- that, '*I will be Rich.*' The important part is to know how to select the right seed, to plant it, give it a proper nurturance, and grow it into a healthy strong tree so that it can start bearing the right kind of fruits and in lots of quantity.

We are what we are because of the seeds of thought we have planted. If we want to be rich, we have to plant the right seed; the seed of mango will not produce an apple. For a harvest of riches, we have to plant the seed for being rich in our minds.

Oops! I forgot. Before we select the seed and plant it, we have to prepare the soil to receive it. Without the soil preparation, the seed will die. So, let us start from the very beginning. Initially, it is the soil preparation that matters.

Prepare the Soil for Seeding

It is our attitude to wealth which holds us back. In the majority of the cases, it does not provide the right kind of soil to plant the seed of wealth. Most of us aspire to be rich but it is our outlook that keeps us poor.

Wealth comes to those who become wealth-conscious. Failure to acquire riches comes to those who are not money conscious. Why do we harbor such a poor attitude towards wealth when we aspire for riches? This is mainly due to how our brain computer was programmed when we were young.

The memory chip in our mind records everything – it records every event, experience, thought, dream or feeling we have ever had. It is an amazing machine. It simultaneously records millions of inputs from our five senses nonstop, 24 hours a day. They are stored in layers and layers, buried deep within our subconscious. Each new layer buries the preceding layer deeper into our subconscious.

Bigger the event, deeper the impression it leaves on our mind. Even the most insignificant of events are recorded and stored; many believe that impressions of our past lives are passed on to us through the genetic code. We are what we are because of the sum total of those past impressions and our personalities and attitudes are defined by these past impressions that are buried deep within our subconscious.

Most of these impressions were recorded when we were very young and had little or no control over them. They were recorded by individuals who had their own limitations of knowledge and human prejudices. They left an indelible mark on our mind because we loved and respected them. They were our parents, teachers and friends whom we trusted because their love for us was unconditional.

Events and thoughts mixed with emotions create the deepest of impressions. It will be wrong to suggest that everything we were taught and all that we experienced in our respective childhoods was wrong.

Some of the knowledge that we gained is invaluable to us. Nothing can substitute the feeling of love, care and concern that was transmitted to us that brings us joy today. But it is wise to know that impressions that form our attitudes today were based on imperfect knowledge.

Another important thing to remember is that the processor in our brain, that interprets the incoming data before recording, was not fully developed when we were young. In many cases, we recorded the wrong results simply because of our faulty interpretations of the events around us.

We judge new events in our lives based on the imperfect information stored in our memory. Our brain processor becomes tainted when it compares new events with our not so perfect recorded data of the past.

Our emotions are the sum total of impressions caused by thoughts and feelings stored in our subconscious, and they are undeniably powerful.

It is our feelings, dominated by the subconscious, that lead to action. While making financial decisions, we are torn between logic and emotions. It is mostly emotions that win.

When feelings become strong within us, they force us to act. Finally, it is action that leads to wealth creation. If we are able to change our thought process, then we can change the outcome of our future. Our destiny is in our hands and we cannot blame it on others.

Limiting Beliefs
that Hold Us Back

Now, let us examine some of the myths about money that were drilled into our subconscious when we were young. You may relate to some of them:

- Money is the root of all evil.

- Behind great wealth there is a crime.

- It takes money to make money.

- Money can't buy you love.

- Money isn't everything.

- It takes hard work to make money.

- The best things in life are free.

- It is easier for a camel to go through the eye of a needle than for a rich man to enter the kingdom of God.

- You can either be an officer and a gentleman or rich.

- Wealthy people are snobbish.

- Money does not grow on trees.

- Money can't buy happiness.

Whew! Even if you believe in a few of them, they are designed to keep you poor for life. In fact, you might even decide to get rid of whatever little money you might have.

Let us examine some of these limiting beliefs to know if they are correct. At one point of time, people believed that the earth was flat. This belief made people behave as though it were flat. As a result, it limited exploration and expansion. Only when it was known that the world is round did Columbus set out to find a sea route to India and in the process discovered America.

The same is true for our limiting beliefs regarding money. So long as we believe in them, they will restrict us in our imagination.

Is money the root of evil?

The answer is a definite no. In most of the cases, it is extreme poverty that drives people to steal, become dishonest and even resort to violence to survive. Money is neutral; it is neither good nor evil. It is, however, a very powerful commodity. When in the hands of the right people, it can do a lot of good or it can become a destructive force when used wrongfully.

It is extreme lust for money that can sometimes make people go wrong. If anything, it is poverty that is evil. It makes people do things that they otherwise will not do. We have to rid the world of poverty from this planet to make it a better place to live in.

Behind great wealth there is a crime

In the initial stages of wealth creation, we do not have access to the right advice as we do not have sufficient money to buy it. Also, at times, our haste to get rich quick makes us cut corners which leads to problems with the taxman or law.

At some point during our growth, dawns the wisdom, that the best and fastest way to create wealth is through a legitimate route. A crime behind every great wealth is a very sweeping statement. In every great endeavor, mistakes are made and a majority of them happen to be genuine.

It's hard to believe that wealth creators like Edison, Carnegie, Warren Buffet, Steve Jobs and Bill Gates had anything to do with crime. This is also true for 99% of the wealth creators who do not fall in the same league.

Money does make money when invested sensibly, but it is only a very small aspect of wealth creation. It is ideas and an educated mind that create wealth and not crime. There are criminals who succeed in the short run but the law invariably catches up.

"Money can't buy me love..."

If there's one thing that stills hums in my mind, it's the lyrics made popular by the Beatles number. Ask any sensible girl – who is also honest – if this assumed correlation between money and love holds true. You will get the right answer.

Someone rightly said, '***Whoever said money can't buy you love doesn't know where to shop.***' The love you have for another, when expressed through something that only money can buy, can bring love in return. Make no mistake on this one.

Money isn't everything

I fully agree with the statement: 'Money isn't everything." There are much more important things in life than money: our families and friends, health, spiritual wellbeing, pursuit of art and culture are definitely more important, amongst many other things. However, money makes it possible to pursue these important things in life. Money provides the freedom to pursue your dreams.

It takes hard work to make money

The rich and the poor have the same number of hours to work. It definitely does not take extraordinary hard work to become rich. Even the poor work hard at what they do, in fact, people who are relatively poor work harder than the rich. The rich because of knowledge work smarter than but not as hard as the poor.

The best things in life are for free

This is very true. Some good things in life do come for free. Like the beautiful sunset or the fresh air we breathe. However, some of the most delightful things in life that we as humans enjoy come with a price tag.

Having money at our disposal does not mean that we cannot enjoy the free things that God bestows on us. With money, we have the power to enjoy both.

It is easier for a camel to go through the eye of a needle than for a rich man to enter the kingdom of God

I will take the privilege to have my own story account for this; I have seen such extreme poverty which I hope no one ever gets subjected to.

Was I ready for spiritual development in those earlier years of poverty? The answer is a definite no. In those initial years, I was just fighting for my survival. God was absent from my conscious mind. I started on my spiritual quest once I was settled in a regular job and had some kind of an income.

My spiritual development has progressed along-with my material advancement. It is never the material world – of being rich or poor – that comes in the way of our spiritual advancement, but the attachment to the material world.

Heaven is not for you, in so far as you're attached to your few possessions; person with an enlightened view to wealth has better chances of making it to heaven.

You can either be an officer and a gentleman or rich

I was invariably imbued with this ideology during my training at the military academy. I instantly identified myself as an officer and a gentleman. This one belief kept me poor for the larger part of my life.

Wars are about financial control and power. Once this knowledge dawned on me, I decided to apply for a premature retirement from the military to follow my destiny.

Wealthy people are snobbish

I have met some of the nicest people who are wealthy. However, it is true that anyone who values their time may appear snobbish when they do not give us adequate attention. Approach a wealth creator with a brilliant thought or an idea and see how attentive they get.

Most enlightened wealth creators are exceedingly humble—they have a spark in them that will kindle a spark in you provided you have the right mindset.

The fault can also lie in our judgment stemming from our own insecure self.

There is a saying, "***When the shoe fits - the shoe is forgotten, when the belt fits - the belt is forgotten, and when the mind is right - for and against are forgotten***." Before passing judgment on others, it is imperative that we have our hearts and minds in the right place.

Money does not grow on trees

On the contrary, money does grow on trees as you further your reading and increase your financial knowledge. The only thing needed is to prepare the soil, plant the right seed, nurture the plant through the initial stages. Once it grows big and strong, it will not only give you all the money you need, but also new seeds to plant more money trees.

Money can't buy happiness

This is very true because happiness is a state of mind. Money, however, can provide you with the freedom to pursue whatever field of activity you may choose, which in turn, helps create a happy state of mind.

It gives you the freedom to travel, go on holidays, get involved in charities, learn new hobbies, indulge in personal development and spend more time with your family. The choice is entirely yours according to your definition of happiness.

Stress-filled, unhappy moments in my life have been – when I could not meet my financial commitments – like paying bills or providing for the basic needs of my family.

The list of attitudes that hold us back from getting rich, discussed in the preceding paragraphs, is not comprehensive. I am sure if you look back at your life, you can compile your own list and find out what holds you back.

Compiling this list may not be as easy as it may seem because we do not understand how our mind works and the power of our attitude. Our inner nature or attitude built over the years resists change. It likes status co to remain and holds us back.

We have layers, and layers of impressions buried deep within our subconscious. Our subconscious guides us what to do. We are like prisoners of our inner nature. If we want to try out new things the data stored in our memory bank tells us this is not possible. It has never been done before. Our teachers and parents warned us against this. If you try this, there is a considerable risk involved. We can't change in spite of our best efforts. We get paralyzed.

If we wish to be successful: managing and training the mind are the most crucial skillsets that are required. We will need to free your perspective from the prejudices of the past.

How to Change Your Attitude

How do you change your attitude? How do you go from 'stay poor' printed in your subconscious to becoming a go-getter who says, "Being rich is your birthright?" Yes, you were born to be rich and it is your birthright.

To make this quantum change in your attitude, you have to take few simple steps. The first thing to do is to become aware of your inner thought process. And how does one become aware? It is simple…meditate!

Please, don't freak out. Most people get confused. They think— to meditate is to get into some tremendous yogic posture and concentrate on the problem till you get the answer to the problem. Nothing can be further from truth.

Meditation means a reversal of the thought process. Our minds are overloaded with continuous inputs from our five senses, 24 hours a day. Even while sleeping, it works all the time chiming in dreams. It is burdened to the extent that it can't think straight.

It is high time you go to a quiet place where there is no disturbance, sit down quietly and turn off your five senses. Now drift inwards towards your mental space and observe what is happening there. Initially, you will see only the top layers - consisting mainly of pressing issues and problems that are worrying your mind.

It takes patience, practice and courage to unravel the inner workings of your mind. To uncover the layers of your mind, you have to become non-judgmental and fearless. The mind will try to put brakes on the flow; there is much fear, hurt and guilt there. It is very hard to uncover memories that cause so much pain. It will need great courage to command the mind to let go of the brakes and allow the buried impressions flow out from the mind.

While reflecting, do not sit in judgement, because you were not responsible for most of the impressions recorded in your subconscious. These events occurred when you had no control over them. They happened during your childhood. Let your thoughts flow out with one part of your mind as a mute witness. It may not happen in the first sitting, but in due course even the most deeply buried impressions will begin to appear.

This is why writers, musicians, painters and other creative people are given such a high pedestal to stand on. It is because each creative idea involves the reversal process of the mind. The creative people can invoke and have access to the deep recesses of their minds, and sometimes, even beyond the mind as we shall learn later.

Our awareness level increases when we start observing our thought process. We begin to understand that most of our actions are as a result of our previous programming. As our level of consciousness increases, we are freed from our pasts and start living, and making decisions in the present.

Increase in awareness will lift the lid on buried emotions, hidden fears and deep-seated myths that you have about money. You will understand the subtle influence that money exerts in each of your relationships, even with your nearest and dearest ones.

Money is the currency of power: it is used to manipulate and control. The person with greater resources uses his or her assets to control the behavior of the other person—whether they are friends, parents, children or spouses. In most cases, this happens at a subconscious level with none of the players fully aware of what is happening. Deep resentment develops in relationships as a result of this gameplay. Money matters are shrouded in mystery and there are layers of emotions that cover our motives.

Some reflection will prove that money is central to all our relationships. It influences many of our choices ranging from whom we marry, our choice of job, where we live to what we wear, eat and experience.

In our society, money is the metaphor for success and achievement. Having it can make us feel worthwhile and not having it can make us feel worthless. We are what we are because of the money we have. Somerset Maugham, put it rightly when he wrote, "***Money is like a sixth sense without which you cannot make complete use of the other five***."

Further reflection will show that men may feel threatened if they earn less than their wives. Men associate money with success, prestige, risk, power and excitement. If a man loses his job, his shoulders will drop as though he has been emasculated and lost his manhood.

A man normally measures his worth to his wife, children and society in purely economic terms. Unemployment can lead to depression, low self-esteem, anger and perceived loss of power. Women on the other hand, look at money as a form of security that gives them freedom and independence. Change in relative earning capacities results in a shift of power dynamics, spending patterns and bedroom politics.

Another area where couples display a wide range of differences is in their ability to tolerate debt. Intimacy is stifled by financial conflict. If there is power imbalance in your financial relationship, there will surely be a similar imbalance in your sexual relationship. In extreme cases, this results in marital tension and relationship breakdowns.

You will be surprised to learn that there are more divorces due to money problems than there are because of sexual ones. Money, not sex, is the last taboo and an intensely private matter. People will discuss their problems of sex openly but when it comes to money they will clamp up even with their spouse. This is because money is power and any discussion regarding money threatens to change the power dynamics in relationships.

In many cases, love becomes a financial transaction. Parents are conditioned to believe that buying things for children is a measure of their love for them. Women feel loved only when their husbands shower them with gifts. Cutting financial resources is a tactic frequently used to establish control in relationships.

Many people offer financial help to gain power and status over others. The recipient, on the other hand, tends to become subservient and in emotional debt. Many people don't even spare themselves and go into a buying spree if they are lonely and depressed.

You must have heard of money strings—they are everywhere and mostly invisible!

Now reflect on your work scene; your financial security depends on your job. If you are fired it, will create havoc for your family. You are forced to succumb to every unreasonable demand of your boss. You cannot speak your mind freely or you may not get the next promotion.

I excelled in my naval career because the driving force there was my financial insecurity. My wellbeing, and that of my family, depended on my doing well in service. I could never speak my mind; deference was a sure way of getting written off. Only when I had built substantial residual income through my real estate investing could I freely express myself. I think I became a much better person and an officer once I gained a sense of financial security.

Money forces us to make compromises at every turn in our lives. Unfortunately, some people cross the barrier and break the law. They steal, don't pay taxes, become corrupt and in extreme cases, even resort to violence and murder. Money corrupts like nothing else.

Reflect on another scenario: what happens if you fall sick or become incapacitated to work? How will you cope? For how long will your insurance pay up? What happens to you or your family that relies on your income? Still many people say that, "money does not matter to them."

Most of us fail to realize that money has a powerful influence on us starting from the moment we're born till we die. We spend most of our waking hours trying to earn a living away from our loved ones. Our free time is spent in thinking about money: How to pay our bills? How to allocate the limited money we have? Whether to buy a new car or a house, go on a holiday, buy new clothes, send our children to better schools or look after our aging parents?

Conflicting requirements and lack of money causes anxiety in the deepest recess of our subconscious. Insecurity and financial pressures make us think and act in ways that are detrimental to those we love and the society at large.

The idea behind silent reflection is to increase awareness regarding money matters. It is to understand that money is the undercurrent of life that drives us. Our physical and spiritual wellbeing depends on it. Decision to acquire wealth and riches is a noble act towards not only us and our families, but the society at large.

Imagine the power of money in enlightened hands and the amount of good it can do: it can provide physical, mental and spiritual freedom. It can free the planet Earth from the ills of poverty that bind millions to a life of misery.

There is no nobler pursuit than the creation of wealth that is done in an enlightened way. It is the forerunner to spiritual development. In fact, spiritual progress is not possible without passing through the material phase and satiation of the basic human needs—which only money can provide.

Look at any religious organization, including the church; they thrive on patronage of the rich. Success in the material world is a prerequisite to entering the spiritual world. So, don't be afraid- it is your destiny to be rich.

There is an energy flow in silent meditation and stillness. Wherever you direct this energy, results will show. It is your mind's energy that decides your destiny and its flow can be controlled through mindfulness and silent observation.

Triggers that Work the Mind

There are principally two triggers that work the mind when it comes to acquiring great wealth. There may be slight variations but fundamentally there are only two triggers.

It is important to understand these triggers because all wealth is generated due to these two triggers. You will need to understand and use these triggers skillfully in order to create wealth. The two triggers are the 'pain' and the 'pleasure' triggers.

Pain comes from deprivation of basic human needs like food, shelter and love. Even the very thought of pain and deprivation can become great motivators that can get us started towards the process of wealth creation.

Pleasure, on the other hand, is fulfillment of desire unsatisfied. Even the thought of pleasure can get our minds excited with all kinds of possibilities and is an equally great motivator to get us started.

Pain pushes us whilst pleasure attracts us towards acquisition of riches. You have to understand what trigger drives you—it can be a bit of both. A little bit of meditation and awareness will help you identify triggers that work your mind. Meditation is nothing else but consciously observing your thoughts without judgement. Once you understand the inner thought process, you will be able to make sound choices in the present and not be driven by programming from the past.

In my case it was extreme poverty that drove me into the arms of spiritual quest to find the answers to my miserable state. For some reason, I bypassed the material stage only to realize at a much later date that my development was incomplete. This realization set me on the path towards attaining material success.

In some ways I am happy that I understood the spiritual values before embarking on the wealth creation process even though it set me back by a couple of decades. Money has given me great satisfaction- to educate my two children in the best of colleges that money could buy. It enabled our family travels around the world and expanded our horizons.

How to Become a Millionaire

The greatest thing about money is the freedom it provides. It gives the freedom of time to explore relationships. Freedom of movement allows us to explore new thoughts, ideas and develop our unique genius. To become an enlightened wealth creator is to have freedom to do what you desire as long as it hurts no one and helps others.

Charity means to help others grow and make them stand on their feet so that they can hold their heads in dignity. Knowledge, education and health are the keys.

Education and the pursuit of knowledge has been the only difference between me and the poor village in India from where I emerged. I hope to acquire all the riches in the world and go back someday to set up an educational system that will empower others to do better than me.

My triggers of pain and pleasure may be different as compared to yours because your circumstances and experience of life are different. Your triggers and dreams are equally worthy. Take time to find them and focus on them.

Do not run after the fruit without sowing the seed first. In doubt- read a little, reflect a little, meditate a little and become aware of the power of the money in your life and the triggers that drive you.

The seed will engender the tree and the fruits, and not the other way round. You are destined to great riches. Being wealthy is your right—you may or may not realize this fact. The world is moving towards materialistic progression. Sooner you understand this fact about money, faster the manifestation of affluence and power will happen in your life.

Make a decision at this very moment that: "I will be rich and enlightened," and you shall be rich and enlightened. Your journey to financial freedom will begin as soon as you sow the seed of prosperity and becoming rich in your mind. It is as simple as that.

Even if one understands the importance of money, it is fear of the unknown and the risky that holds us back. No one has ever succeeded in life or created wealth without taking risks. Whether it is the decision to get married, start a business, invest in a property or choose a career; there are anticipation of the unknown. A sports person or an artist has to decide if they have sufficient talent to pursue their dreams or join the rest of mankind by taking a less risky option.

There is 'fog of war' in every decision in life. No one has a crystal ball to see the future. The worst thing in life is to freeze because of that fear of the unknown. When it comes to money and our financial future, this fear becomes irrational. Let us examine the nature of fear and how we can overcome it to become truly rich.

Fear is the Biggest Enemy of Wealth Creation

That fear festering in your mind is the biggest threat to the seed of wealth creation that you have planted in your mind; it is like a weed that has to be removed before you can succeed.

Fear is a distressing emotion aroused by impending danger, evil, pain, etc., irrespective of whether the threat is real or imagined.

Fear is a hard-wired emotion, triggered by our subconscious. As human beings, we naturally fear everything that is unfamiliar to us and anything from our past that has resulted in feelings of pain. These feelings signal our brain, which drives our actions in such a manner that causes us to avoid pain at all costs. We will instinctually go to great lengths to prevent circumstances that bring about fear and the stress that is created within us through that fear.

We are afraid of fear because we are afraid of pain. This creates a very real problem for us, in that; we are instinctively driven away from just about everything that would result in the creation of our own financial independence.

Fear will always overwhelm everything that might bring about real change in our lives- it is unavoidable. It is in the nature of our brains to protect us from pain unless we make a conscious choice to achieve greater reward than the resulting pain brought about by what we fear.

DOUBT, FEAR, and ANXIETY are the three demons that bring our progress to an abrupt halt, right at the point when we are about to make a decision that has the potential to change our lives. Doubt creeps in and causes the fear, which in turn, causes the anxiety. The three can strike at lightning speed and freeze our decision-making capacity.

The demon of fear is, without a doubt, the biggest obstacle in our minds that does not allow us to nourish the seed of wealth. It is the fear of failure of losing all that we have achieved so far. It is the fear of criticism and ridicule. It is the fear of losing love and respect of our near and dear ones. It is always this irrational fear that holds us back from achieving greatness and financial success.

What is the source of this fear?

What is it that causes us to freeze and lose our senses, rationality and the power to act? The primary cause of this debilitating demon is ignorance. Knowing this truth will set us free. That, in itself, is a beautiful truth.

You must understand that there is only one thing to be set free from and that is ignorance. If you analyze carefully, it is always the lack of knowledge, and the understanding of things and situations that causes fear. Let me explain: prior to the age of Enlightenment, thunder and lightning, like most unknown forces, were misunderstood and proved to be a source of great fear in the minds of people. Tumultuous nights usually scared people out of their wits, they did not comprehend what was happening. They would believe the Gods to be angry and felt guilty of their wrongdoings. It left a very deep impression of fear on their minds.

These days when science has explained the true nature of thunder and lightning, occurrences and fluctuations in weather do not cause any anxiety or fear in our minds. It leaves no impression whatsoever. We go about our daily works as if nothing has happened. It is a non-event. *Fear burns in the fire of knowledge*. Likewise, if you have the right financial knowledge, you will not suffer from fear of failure.

Similarly, our fears predominate due to the layers and layers of wrong inputs and impressions stored in our subconscious. These impressions were formed as a result of the education system that was designed in the industrial age: designed in an age where only few were privileged and the rest were trained mentally and professionally to be at their service.

Our parents and teachers, whom we loved and admired, were part of the same education system. They unknowingly passed the same knowledge down to us: become professionals, become doctors, engineers, accountants and lawyers. Get a job in a good company, work hard and be successful. No one taught us to be wealth creators. No one taught us the skills to be wealth creators.

Even the media, influencing public opinion profoundly, is a product of that old thought. We can't blame them. They were educated in the same school of thought as most of us. They imbibed the fear of God into us. The economy is going downhill. Next year, there will be a recession: they rattle rising unemployment figures, oil prices, inflation rate, foreign debt, national debt and make comparisons with the great depression of the thirties, when everyone seemed to have lost their homes and jobs.

Fear, greed and sensationalism sells—rationality does not. No doubt we're so afraid! Who would like to jump on to the bandwagon of uncertainties? Why take risks when you can get a decent job and survive? Fear is programmed in our memory chip in form of a blueprint that dictates our financial lives.

How to Overcome Fear?

We have to erase and rewrite that program if we have to succeed. Knowledge helps us to examine these fears and erase them from our systems.

Now look at the facts: our mindsets were created in a world that was poor. This was a time when there was a distinction between the privileged and the poor. These economic positions in life seldom changed. Either you were born rich or you worked for the rich. This has all changed now.

The world is moving forward at an unprecedented pace. Despite the doomsayers' prediction by the media, the world is on a projected trajectory of great material advancement. You have to just assess history, starting from the industrial revolution, to understand the financial progress made by mankind. This pace has accelerated in the past 50 years and will increase in manifolds as the information age progresses.

There might be slight aberrations but the writing is on the wall for anyone to see. The wealth of the world is about to explode as never seen before—

are you going to be a part of this expansion or get left behind?

At present, there are less than 0.1% wealth creators on this planet. This is going to change very rapidly because this advancing information age makes it possible to impart knowledge. Are you ready to acquire that new knowledge that will burn your fears and set you on path of great wealth?

Expand Your Mind State

You have made a decision to become an enlightened wealth creator; else you would not be reading this book. This is great...but be warned! Your inner nature is very powerful and strong; it is fortified by millions and millions of past impressions.

Our minds are like an elastic band: if the new force is not applied, it will try to snap you back and restore to its original position. You will need to keep applying the pressure of knowledge and burn your fears till you break free.

This is the stage where permanent transformation takes place and you do not go back to your original position. It is as though the rocket fueled by knowledge puts you into outer space beyond the pull of gravity. There is a saying that, "**Once your mind expands it never goes back to its original state.**" You will have to keep applying the pressure of Knowledge incessantly, till you find yourself in an expanded state of mind.

A rocket burns 90% of its fuel during its take off stage: once it defies gravity, very little energy is needed to keep it running. The same is true for a mind that wants to grow to an expanded state to create wealth.

All information that is recorded in our memory passes through a processor in our minds before it is recorded. The previously stored data that is recorded in our systems interferes with the processor as it analyzes incoming data. We have the capacity to change our blueprint by first erasing the old blue print by burning it in the light of new knowledge.

As the old data gets progressively removed from our systems, its interference reduces, and the capacity of our mind's processor improves. The process is very slow as there are layers and layers of files accumulated in our system. Some of these are like viruses that continuously affect the capacity of our processor to analyze data correctly.

It is a catch 22 situation: our processors are affected by the same files it is trying to analyze, which makes the task very slow and tedious. However, we can make a quantum jump in our processing capability by upgrading our processors, by increasing our financial, emotional and spiritual intelligence.

Financial Intelligence

An intellect that is honed financially helps one see opportunities that they otherwise would have not. These opportunities are seen with the mind. An unknowing fool will throw a gem away thinking it is another stone; a wealth creator will see an opportunity to make money which an untrained mind cannot see.

Financial Intelligence is the third eye which opens doors to opportunities where none exist. It creates new opportunities. That is why they say 'rich invent money.' An untrained mind, on the other hand, can create extreme poverty that lasts generations by teaching it to their families.

Financial intelligence not only creates wealth, it sustains it. There are innumerable stories of professional sportsmen who made millions during their playing years only to become bankrupt within a decade. Mike Tyson, a heavyweight champion, is one such example. He earned millions during his lifetime but is now bankrupt.

You must have also heard about lottery winners who are back to where they started within five years of winning the lottery ticket.

I was recently reading an article on the descendants of Hyder Ali and Tipu Sultan who are today penniless. They are members of families who ruled over half of India few generations ago. Why is it that these families lost their wealth? There are other families who not only sustain but grow their fortunes over generations.

The world changes, markets go up and down, technologies change, economies boom and crash. The families who survive are those that make the efforts it takes to develop their financial intelligence, which allows them to adjust to the changes and also helps find new opportunities to succeed in this changing world. They also take the trouble to teach and transmit this intelligence to their younger generations and hence, are able to sustain their wealth for generations to come.

What is Financial IQ?

There are many facets of financial intelligence. It is about understanding assets and liabilities, capital growth and cash flows, passive income as against earned income, good debt and bad debt and making money work for you instead of you working for money. It is also about tax savings and protecting your assets including intellectual property rights.

Let us examine some of these aspects in greater detail.

Assets and Liabilities

An asset, as explained by Robert Kiyosaki in his book 'Rich Dad Poor Dad', is something which puts money into your pocket and liability is something that takes money out of your pocket. By this definition your house, car, boat, golf set and other luxury items that you buy (thinking they are assets) are in actual fact liabilities. All these so-called assets take money out of your pocket. Most of these depreciate in value (except may be your house,) and are high maintenance items that cost money out of your pocket.

Most of us think that we are buying assets, but in actuality, we buy liabilities that keep us poor. This does not imply that one should not buy these things that make us feel nice and good about life: one must buy them only once sustainable wealth has been created by first purchasing income-producing assets.

The real assets are businesses, investment properties, shares, bonds, etc., that put money into your pockets and also appreciate in value. To create wealth is to buy income producing assets such as real estate, businesses and paper assets.

Capital Gain and Cash flow

Wealth is created through a combination of capital growth and cash flow. Capital growth creates long-term wealth whereas cash flow sustains it in the short term and a balance between the two is needed to sustain and fuel the growth.

Short-sighted people only go for cash flow to fund their current needs. On the other hand, there are long-term investors (especially those who invest in properties) who get into serious trouble by not understanding the importance of cash flow. A sensible combination of the two is needed to grow financially.

Good Debt and Bad Debt

People are scared of taking debt for business expansion and investments as it causes a lot of stress. At the same time, they are not afraid of taking loans to buy cars or to go on a holiday.

Financially intelligent people know that creating debts for buying income-producing assets is a prerequisite for growing rich. A good debt is when money is borrowed to create money. Just like the bank: banks take money deposits from us at a lower interest rate and loan it back to businesses or for purchasing properties at a much higher interest rate. They make money on the difference, as can anyone.

The simple trick is to borrow cheap and create an asset that pays more. Bad debts are the ones that you borrow at high interest rate and use for buying assets that depreciate or produce less, or no income.

Make Money Work for You

The best definition that defines being rich is: "***In case you stop working today because of ill health/ accident or voluntary retirement then for how long will your savings sustain your current life style.***" In some cases, it may be just a few days or at best a couple of months- this means you are poor.

In other cases, it may be a couple of years. A tad better situation but is certainly not a healthy one! You will be rich if you can sustain your lifestyle adjusted for inflation, indefinitely.

The super-rich can not only sustain their present lifestyle but they make it better, and also have surplus income to reinvest so that their net wealth increases with each passing year.

This can only happen when you have a large component of your money coming from passive income in the form of rents from commercial/residential real estate, dividends from shares, intellectual property rights or interest earned from deposits. In other words, it is money working for you even when you sleep or are on holiday. In case of a job, the money will stop flowing the moment you stop working.

Saving on Taxman's Dollars

You may or may not realize this, but the most outflow of money from your pocket, during your lifetime, is the money paid in taxes. In many countries, taxes can be more than 50% of the income earned. These include the GST, Income Tax, Custom Duties, Excise Duties, Service Tax, Sales Tax, Capital Gains Tax, Stamp Duties and Estate Duties etc.

You may not even be aware of some of the taxes you pay because they are cut at the very source— before you get paid or they get added to the price of goods that you buy on a daily basis. If you add them all up, taxes can take away anything ranging from 40-75% of all that you earn.

Financially intelligent people use investment vehicles and tax saving strategies to save on these taxes. Money saved from taxes through proper planning and invested sensibly can make even a modest earner into a millionaire many times over.

Most financially uneducated people will try and hide their income to save on taxes, and eventually, get in trouble with the law. They will try and save dollars by not consulting an astute accountant and setting up proper structures to save legitimately on taxes.

To grow financially, one has to provide their income details and their turnover: when you do that, you become liable to pay tax. Proper tax planning – not tax avoidance – is the route financially intelligent people take.

Structures for Asset Protection and Tax Planning

This is a very important component of financial intelligence. You should protect your wealth even as you earn. Things, sometimes, can go wrong even with the right knowledge and intentions because no one can have full control over their environment or future events. There is an unknown element in each financial decision we take.

Rich people set up proper structures for asset protection and tax planning before they start. Yes, there is a cost involved in setting up these structures at the beginning, especially at a time when the business or the entity is not generating any income. Normally the cost involved is very small and will pay itself hundred times over if set up correctly. It will also make you sleep better at night.

Risk and Risk Management

Most people refrain from starting a business or investing somewhere because they feel that there is a huge risk involved. What appears like a risk to an untrained mind is like a cake walk for the financially intelligent. This is because they understand those risks and take adequate steps to insure that risk.

I sailed around the world in a 40 ft. yacht. My friends and family thought I had put myself at great risk in such a small boat but I had trained hard and was a knowledgeable sailor. I understood and respected the sea in all its moods. To me, sailing that boat was safe and an enjoyable experience that enriched me as a person.

Life itself is a risk! The fact that we are born and continue to live is a risky business. We travel by cars and airplanes that can meet with accidents. The human body is fragile. It can give in to cancer, heart failure or a stroke at any stage.

Then there are natural disasters that can strike us at any moment: earthquakes, tsunamis, volcanoes, fires or even a strike from an asteroid can take our lives away in an instance.

Added to this, man has created enough disasters for himself in the form of wars, nuclear power, global warming and terrorism. We cover our risks in daily life by taking prudent decisions and by insuring our health, life and property.

The same can be done in our financial lives. In today's world, every financial risk can be insured. There is a premium involved but this can be an expense that can be taken into account into the cost of running a business or investment. Financially intelligent people not only take out insurances, but also have an exit policy in place for every decision they take. They have business structures in place so that their personal wealth is not touched even if businesses or investments fail.

Robert Kiyosaki rightly put it: "***It is never the business or an investment that is risky. It is always the businessman or the investor who is the risk.***" It is our lack of financial knowledge that causes the risk. We get carried away by our emotions of fear and greed, which cause the risk. Risk can be controlled and even eliminated through proper knowledge and insurance.

The biggest risk in life is to remain poor and to have no assets. An even bigger risk in life is to think that someone else will come to our rescue in the hour of need: be it the government, family or friends.

The best thing in life is to rely on our own strength and take steps to become not only financially secure but rich. We have a responsibility towards our family and loved ones to cater for their wellbeing, growth and emergencies in life. The real risk is in not taking timely action to make them financially secure. Avoiding risks to improve one's financial future is just an excuse.

Key Skills of Financially Intelligent People

Financially intelligent people have certain key skills that make them rich. Unfortunately, these key skills are not the focus of what is taught in our schools and colleges.

Creative Thinking

We live in an information age. Most of the times, our minds are overloaded with information; be it the television, the internet, mobile phones or many books and magazines. There is so much information available and very little time to process and digest it. Creative thinking suffers as a result.

A problem solving and creative mind knows where to look for information, and process the data towards a predetermined useful end. An undisciplined mind will waste hundreds of hours in non-productive conversation over the phone or surfing the net lacking focus.

Discipline and focus release the mind from information overload. Only a restive, inward looking and a meditative mind can think creatively and solve problems.

Negotiating

In life, to get what we want, we have to negotiate. We have to get the other party to agree to our terms and conditions. We have to have the skills to change their initial responses: from a "No" to a

"Yes." We have to learn the art of compromising for the betterment of both parties.

Communicating

There can be no successful business transaction without proper communication skills. Forget about business development, even marriages and friendships rescind when there is a communication breakdown. You will not achieve your desired results, so long as you are not able to communicate your point of view.

Selling and Marketing

For most people, selling a product or an idea has horrible connotations. It involves rejection, which most people find hard to swallow. The basic truth is that there can be no wealth creation without selling a product or an idea. Profits are generated and encashed once they're sold.

You cannot be successful in any walk of life without being skilled in selling. When you walk into a job interview, you are selling your skills, talents and personality. Even successful dating involves selling your charm, beauty, inner qualities and character.

It is not selling that is difficult: it is the fear of rejection that one has to conquer. Ask any successful entrepreneur and he will tell you that marketing and selling together constitute the oxygen of any business.

Mathematical Mind

Investment and business is about numbers. Basic knowledge of mathematics and accounting is essential to develop a financial mindset. There is no calculus or higher mathematics involved, but basic knowledge is essential.

Emotional Intelligence

We are human beings and emotions play a big part in how we react to the events occurring in our lives. Unfortunately, we cannot control everything that is happening in the world but we can control our reactions to the events that affect us.

Money can be a very emotional thing. If you don't believe me, just visit a stock exchange market and dispassionately observe people and their behavior. How fear and greed take over our rational thinking, how jealous and angry we can get when it comes to money!

Lack of an emotional intelligence causes internal friction in our minds, which saps our energy to do more productive work. There is an internal dialogue which takes place within our minds continuously. There is strife and irritation in our heads if our internal value system is in conflict with our conscious mind. It is only when both are in tune that there is peace within, and our energy levels explode.

What is Emotional Intelligence?

Our emotions emerge from the subconscious. Emotional intelligence accounts for our ability to change unconscious reactions to a conscious response. It means: to perceive and understand emotion, integrate emotion to facilitate thought, and to regulate emotions to promote personal and financial growth.

There is a verse in the Upanishads (sacred Indian text) that states, "If you know a lump of clay then you will know about all the clay in the universe." This means that if you know and understand your own mind, then you will understand all the minds in the universe. All minds function in a similar manner. All our basic human and emotional needs are the same.

To improve our emotional intelligence, we have to bring more and more of our subconscious into conscious examination. Knowledge of the self is the most important step towards improving our emotional intelligence.

Wealth Creation is 90% psychology and only 10% strategy. We have to make internal changes and adjustments to our thinking process that is governed to a very large extent through our emotions, before we can go out and start making money. Changing our psychological foundations is the difficult part, once that is done, creating wealth is a cakewalk.

Spiritual Intelligence

It is essential to understand that we do not live only on one plane of existence. Firstly, there is the material world which we can see, feel and understand. This is the gross or outer cover of life. We aspire for material success and possessions in this world.

Then there is the mind which has two parts: the conscious and the subconscious part. We can't see it, but we know it is there because we can think and dream. The reality of this mind can be entirely different from the real world because it can imagine, dream and be creative.

Finer still is our spirit. Science can't prove it, but we know it is there. It is the unifying force of the universe. It is the underlying principle of life and existence. It unites and not divides. It connects everything in this universe.

At the level of the spirit, we are all one without any differentiation. It is an all-knowledgeable force that permeates into every living or non-living thing. It is also the source of all joy and bliss in this universe. You may call it soul, God or by any other name. It is a reality we cannot deny because at some level we can sense it.

Human spirit is the creative life force of this universe. Most people do not realize that whatever happens in the material world is the printout of the happenings in our spiritual and mental world. Creative people understand this fact and they dip their minds into the cosmos' intelligence to solve their problems and get new ideas.

What is Spiritual Intelligence?

The best definition of spiritual intelligence that I have found is by Frances Vaughan, who states:

"*Spiritual intelligence is concerned with the inner life of mind and spirit and its relationship to being in the world. It emerges as consciousness evolves into an ever-deepening awareness of matter, life, body, mind, soul, and spirit. Spiritual intelligence, then, is more than individual mental ability. It appears to connect the personal to the transpersonal and the self to spirit. Spiritual intelligence goes beyond conventional psychological development. In addition to self-awareness, it implies awareness of our relationship to the transcendent, to each other, to the earth and all beings. Spiritual intelligence opens the heart, illuminates the mind, and inspires the soul, connecting the individual human psyche to the underlying ground of being. Spiritual intelligence can be developed with practice and can help a person distinguish reality from illusion. It may be expressed as love, wisdom, and service."*

There are two important things to understand: even the subtlest of movement in the spiritual mind can change things dramatically for the better in the subconscious and the conscious mind, with a resulting effect in the material world.

A thought impulse originating from the spirit can change our whole life. We only have to learn how to trigger that impulse. Secondly, as we gain spiritual intelligence, it harmonizes us with the rest of nature because it a unifying force. This is very important to us in the material world.

It is our sense of conflict in the material world that saps our energy. If we are in harmony then a powerful energy source explodes within us. This has as huge impact on our success in the material world, which is why developing spiritual intelligence is so important to our success.

Abundance of the Universe

Most people feel that to become rich you have to compete for the limited resources that are available in the material world. The act to acquire something in the material world means that you are denying something to the weaker. They abhor the idea that the rich exploit the helpless poor to build their financial empire, which creates a feeling of guilt that holds us back from becoming rich.

Many politicians have won elections exploiting this feeling of guilt and using the theory of social injustice. There is nothing further from the truth because the universe is not limited but abundant. There is no shortage. It is limited only by our restrictive minds.

Our universe is fundamentally abundant. It holds not millions, but billions of undiscovered thoughts, ideas and resources. Each thought, each idea can find resources that are worth billions of dollars.

Just look at the past: there was no television, radio or telecommunications industry before radio waves were discovered. Today, these are huge industries churning out billions of dollars and providing millions of jobs. The person who discovered this one idea – uncovered one secret of the universe – made millions of people wealthy. He did not take anything from the poor but elevated many from the poverty trap.

The same is true of nuclear energy, internet and thousands of new technologies and millions of ideas that are yet to be discovered. Even a very small idea can generate millions for us. We have to open our minds to understand the abundance of the universe.

"Out of abundance he took abundance and still abundance remained."

- Upanishads

The only truth about the universe: it is abundant!

If we embrace such an attitude, blessings and opportunities will follow. It is only limited minds that think that we compete for resources. It is the crab mentality that insinuates pulling others down to succeed.

In fact, truth is just the opposite. We succeed when we help others to succeed. There is abundance in this universe.

Darwin's theory of 'Survival of the fittest' only applies to the animal world. We humans have risen from rest of the animals because of our ability to co-operate and form societies for greater good. It is only fools who think that we are fighting for limited resources in order to survive.

Understanding abundance grows our financial, emotional and spiritual intelligence.

Honesty and Integrity

It is impossible to create long term wealth through dishonest means. The moment you become dishonest you fall out of sync with humanity and the rule of law. You will waste your creative energy fighting with your business partners, competitors, taxmen, customers and employees. Lies breed more lies. Truth and law will eventually catch up with you.

By being honest and leading a life of integrity, you will not only avoid any potential conflicts but generate goodwill that will have a multiplier effect in your wealth creation process. It is difficult to understand why people cheat at times and get violent and get in trouble with the law. In the process, they get entangled in fights, time consuming and expensive law suits, when it takes only miniscule effort to be honest and develop a financial intelligence to create wealth.

Getting Out of the Comfort Zone

To become rich is not easy and convenient. Getting rich can be very hard work. ***If you are willing to do only what is easy, life will be hard. But if you are willing to do what is hard, life will be easy.*** The rich are always willing to take difficult decisions and act on them whereas the poor take the easy and convenient way out.

To become rich is to step out into the unknown and conquer fear. Exploring new thoughts and ideas and incorporating them into our lives means getting out of that comfort zone we are accustomed to.

Each time you step out of your comfort zone, you conquer uncertainty and fear. This expands the size of your comfort zone. The size of your 'comfort zone' equals the size of your 'wealth zone'. By expanding your comfort zone, you will expand the size of your income and wealth.

The more comfortable you are in your little cocoon, fewer risks you will be willing to take and fewer opportunities will come your way. The more contracted you become with fear, fewer people you will meet, and fewer new strategies will you try.

If you are willing to stretch and expand your financial, emotional and spiritual intelligence, the size of your comfort zone will increase and you will attract and hold more income and wealth. The minute you become comfortable, you stop growing.

A moment of fear freezes you for eternity. Being comfortable and fearful has killed more ideas, opportunities, more action and more growth than everything else combined.

The human mind is the greatest soap-opera script writer in history. It plays and replays the greatest dramas—full of tragedies and disasters that never happened and probably never will. Mark Twain said it best: "*I've had thousands of problems in my life, most of which never happened.*"

Training and managing our minds out of fear and worries is the most important skill that we will ever develop. We have the power to run our thoughts. We will turn into a failure if we allow our uncontrolled thoughts to dictate our actions.

We have the ability to cancel any thought that does not support our growth process. We have to choose and install self-empowering thoughts. We have the power to control our minds and choose the actions that make us mentally, emotionally, financially and spiritually strong.

Robert Allen said something very profound: "**No thought lives in our head rent- free**." This means if we have fear and negativity in our minds, we will have to pay in terms of money, in energy, in time, in health and in happiness. If we have to move forward then we have to control and expand our mental state. We have to overcome our hesitancy and fears and re-write the script that governs our life.

You can be a millionaire in the next 24 months or sooner, if you can overcome the fear that holds you back.

Can We Totally Eliminate Fear through Knowledge?

The answer is no. The process to perfect our financial, emotional and spiritual intelligence may take years. Our knowledge and training can reduce fear to a very large extent but cannot totally eliminate it.

There will always be grey areas in our knowledge and fear of the unknown will make us hesitant from taking an action.

Act we must, despite our fears, because without action there is no wealth. Every decision in this world is taken with incomplete knowledge. We may try and cover most ground to reduce risk but complete knowledge of the future events and forestalling results is impossible.

We have to make decisions that affect our financial futures in spite of the fear that shackles our minds. This is where the leap of faith comes in: our spiritual intelligence gives us that faith. Courage means to act in spite of fear.

President Franklin D. Roosevelt said it best in his inaugural speech of 1933: *"The only thing we have to fear is fear itself."*

Fear is a natural emotion, and one which we experience with any endeavor we make, as long as we are alive. However, the choice to overcome that fear is ours to make, and will be the determining factor as to whether we fail or we succeed.

I remember seeing a war film wherein a soldier approaches his officer and confesses: "**Sir, I am terribly scared of going into combat.**" The officer gives the soldier a knowing look and says so wisely, "**They must have forgotten to tell you**

in training school that courage only comes after you face your fears."

Where there is success, there will always be the threat of failure. You can't have a victory when there is no threat of defeat—that's just reality. If this was not true, there would be no such thing as competitive sports: there would be no Olympics, there would be no Super Bowl, and there would be no Heavyweight Champion titles. Success is about defeating failure.

Knowledge is a big help in eliminating fear. But no one acts out of perfect knowledge. There is an element of uncertainty in every decision we make. It is not necessary to try and get rid of fear; success is about acting in spite of our fear.

Fears, when examined in the light of knowledge, are no longer fears. The impressions of financial fear and loss that are so deeply embedded in our hearts and mind begin to reduce with an increase in our financial, emotional and spiritual intelligence. Once this irrational fear is removed from the heart and the mind, the path for gaining riches is cleared.

It can take years to first erase and then rewrite the script in our subconscious that will set us onto path of wealth creation. Our fears and attitudes come in the way of our knowledge progression because they contaminate our processors.

If we had better attitudes and fewer fears, then our mind's processor will not be tainted; acquisition of new thoughts and ideas will be that much better. Once we have more knowledge, then we can better understand our attitudes and fears that cause hindrance in our journey of becoming rich.

The endless cycle of filtration and purifying of knowledge continues: we move from less knowledge to more knowledge and break one chain at a time that ties us to poverty. This can take an awfully long time. Fortunately, there are ways and means to short cut the process if we make a conscious effort to hasten the process.

How to Re-wire to Become an Enlightened Millionaire

The first step to becoming an enlightened millionaire is to get the mindset of a millionaire. **Process of wealth creation is 90% psychology and only 10% strategy**. Most people fail to become rich because they want to learn the strategy and not focus on changing their psychology.

To be a winner, you have to have the mindset of a winner. The inner change has to precede the external outcome. We have known this since the time we were kids: a certain set of rules enlisted by our parents, teachers and peers need to be followed. We believed in them because they were given to us in love and in good faith. Some of the rules that were ingrained in us were from people whose mindsets were steeped in poverty. We can't blame them because one or two generations back, most of our families were poor and struggling to survive.

As the world moves towards greater prosperity, we have to learn the new set of rules that govern the rich. The new rules are easy to learn only if you have an open mind to learn and succeed. We have to rewrite the script, or order a new set of rules that govern our lives.

It is not sufficient to get rid of the old impressions from our minds – it is only the first step. The old script was a baggage that held us back from becoming rich and forbade us from living life to its full potential.

To succeed, we have to re-write the old script to that of the 'Enlightened Millionaire' in our minds. This is the inner principle of wealth creation. Once the new script is written, it is a point of no return. You can never be middle-class or poor again even if you lose your entire wealth and have to restart from a scratch.

The millionaire mindset once achieved, is a non-destructive commodity. It stays with you for life. You can lose your millions but you will always bounce back. You are a millionaire because of your mindset.

Re-write the Script from Your Heart

The motivation to re-write the script has to originate from the heart because the mind has its own set of limitations— it is always the heart that rules. Whenever there is a conflict between the heart and the mind, it is always the heart that wins. A transformational change can occur only if it comes from the heart. Incremental increase of knowledge can take place in the mind but transformation of the mind can take place only if the heart is involved.

The heart, as we know it, is our subconscious. How can we involve our subconscious into the wealth creation process? To do that, we have to understand what triggers our heart and soul. We have so many desires buried within our subconscious. We have to simply uncover and trigger one or more of these desires into the wealth creation process.

To involve the heart means to find the predominant motivating triggers and activating them. You cannot live someone else's dream— you have to find your own.

The secret of wealth creation lies in finding your own triggers that drive your heart and soul. The nobler your trigger, the greater are your chances of success. A higher and better cause gets more people involved and your chances towards success increases exponentially.

A callous desire normally results in conflicting situations with a lesser chance of success. However, there is nothing wrong in following any of your dreams because once a dream is satisfied; there is always a next dream that will trigger you towards greater cause and effect. It is an evolutionary process. It is however, prudent on what you set your heart on and as Emerson rightly pointed out, "*it surely will be yours*."

To understand our triggers, we have to apply the *S.S.S* formula explained by Ron Holland in his book Talk and Grow Rich. According to him, to understand our subconscious we have to follow **SILENCE, STILLNESS AND SOLITUDE**. The secret to understanding these triggers of our mind lies in meditation – in silence, stillness and solitude or the S.S.S. When you become quiet, it just dawns on you.

Sometimes, an external stimulus is needed to activate the internal process... much like the process of falling in love. It is the beauty of an external person that activates love and desire in our hearts.

Similarly, experience of suffering can ignite compassion in our hearts. At times by putting ourselves in situations and gaining the right stimuli, we can understand the triggers that operate within our subconscious.

You will be able to re-write the '**enlightened millionaire**' script much faster if you understand your dreams and inner motivation. So take time out to understand these dreams and write them on a piece of paper—it will hasten the process. If you know your objective, then the path to success becomes easier to tread on.

The Butterfly Effect

To bring about internal change in our attitude, we have to understand the butterfly effect. The phrase refers to the idea that the flapping of a butterfly's wings might create tiny changes in the atmosphere that ultimately cause a tornado to appear (or prevent a tornado from appearing.)

The flapping wing represents a small change in the initial condition of the system, which causes a chain of events leading to large-scale phenomena. This implies that a small change in the initial condition may produce large variations in the long-term behavior of the system.

We do not have to do anything spectacular to help change our script to an 'enlightened millionaire's mindset,' but we can make small changes to alter the initial condition that can change the long term trajectory of our lives. In the succeeding paragraphs we will discuss some suggestions that can trigger a butterfly effect. You may apply some or all of them to change the outcome of your life.

Control the Inputs to Your Mind

To change the script of our life, we have to understand how the script is written in the mind. The script in the mind is written through thoughts, words, feelings and actions. Each one of them is very important as they leave indelible impressions on the mind. If we can learn to control our thoughts, words, feelings and actions in the present, then we have the power to change our future.

Power of Thoughts and Words

Thoughts are subtle but important because they are the starting point of the process. But once they become words, they have tremendous impact on both our internal and external reality. If you don't believe me, just call someone a bastard and your teeth will come out. Similarly, words of love and kindness will evoke a totally different – but positive – response.

Words, both written and oral, have tremendous power. They leave a deep impression on the mind. We are responsible for our thoughts and words and have to learn to control them. To have the millionaire's mindset, we have to snap out of any negative thought or action.

We have to read or listen to the words of successful and enlightened wealth creators. We have to place ourselves in their company and associate with them so that their words may influence us and change our script.

To illustrate this point: write down the names of five people with whom you spend your maximum time. Now, study their profile. Are they rich... entrepreneurs? Are they wealth creators? Or are they limited in their vision of job security? If you hang around with poor, negative and unsuccessful people then that is what the future beholds for you. You are writing the script of poverty.

To write the script of an enlightened wealth creator, you have to seek the right company to influence your mind. You have to change your reading habits and listen to lectures and tapes of highly successful people. You have to learn to speak the language of the rich.

Your script change will gain added momentum when words of success and positivity start flowing from your pen and mouth. The words you think, write and speak have greater impact on your mind than the words you receive from others.

Initially, the control of thoughts and words will look artificial and irksome. It may not come naturally but it can be done. It has to be a conscious effort. You have to start by watching our thoughts and words, and speak with good purpose only.

Through a change in your reading habits and allowing your mind to be influenced by the right associations, you can accelerate the process and completely change your script to that of an enlightened millionaire. It is a small change in the initial condition that is required to create the 'Butterfly Effect'. And once the effect takes place, it becomes a part of your inner nature.

There can be no Change without Action

Thoughts and words have to manifest into action lest there will be no change. Moreover, action and events in the external world leave a far greater impact on your mind than thoughts and words.

Thoughts are the starting point. They are subtle but create the least impact. Once they manifest into words, they create a much greater impact on the mind. And once words manifest into action, they have the most powerful impact on our minds and the outer world.

To understand this point, let us take the example of an inventor; he thinks of a new invention or product. It is just a concept in his mind. He does not wish to pursue the idea further. It dies a natural death. If he decides to writes a paper on the subject and speak at a few seminars, it not only clarifies his thought process but also starts influencing the minds of others. Now if he takes action to create the new product, then it will impact his future in financial terms but will also leave an impact on those who use or associate with the product.

Actions, though a result of thoughts and words, can prove to be a more powerful instrument of change, as they have a greater impact on the script.

A huge number of people, who read the right kind of books, listen to tapes and attend seminars but take no action. They wish to acquire complete knowledge and eliminate risk before embarking on the process of wealth creation. That perfect situation never comes because what future beholds, no one knows—it is always full of uncertainties.

An educated mind can eliminate some eventualities but, "the fog of war will always remain." All successful commanders know when to act despite being provided with limited information on the enemy. Inaction certainly leads to defeat. The same is true in the world of finance.

If you do not act then you cannot make any money. There is saying: "*once you put your money in line, knowledge will come that much faster*." There is no faster way to rewrite the enlightened millionaire's script than to take action. There is no teacher like experience. Think big but start small. Learn to take a few successful steps before you can start to run.

Knowledge + Action = Wealth

Action is the key. Without action, all your knowledge turns to waste. Be bold and take action. Boldness has genius, power and magic.

Whatever your inspiration or dream—act on it. The most fundamental principle of wealth creation is to take action. No one can ever reach the stage of complete knowledge to overcome fear.

All wealth creators have to learn to manage fear. In every decision you take, there will be an element of uncertainty. There has to be a leap of faith as the information required for decision making is never adequate. Act, you must, in good faith and intelligence! Inaction will keep you tied to poverty.

Once you start taking action, your experience and confidence will increase. There is no better teacher than experience. A few successful steps will change your future. You will rewrite wealth script ten times faster with action.

Feelings make your Words and Actions Stronger

Words when spoken with feelings are a hundred times stronger than those spoken with no heart in them. Have you enjoyed a song that has been sung with passion? It takes a totally new dimension. The same is true for action when it is backed by positive emotion.

When there is joy in action, there is no burden on the task at hand. If the heart is not there, it becomes a tedious job. To rewrite your script your heart has to be in it. Without feelings, there will be no joy or beauty in your script. It will be very difficult to rewire.

Uncovering the power of your emotions will release a tidal wave of change in your life. When there is feeling of love in your words and actions, you will be transformed.

To understand your genius and passion, you have to be still. Through silent introspection, self-reflection and meditation you increase your self-awareness. As your self-awareness increases, you will understand what your heart really wants. Don't chase the artificial or what the world wants you to be. Be true to yourself and your inner beliefs and success will follow you.

Clarity of Purpose

There has to be clarity of purpose when rewriting your script or it will be unintelligible. If there is no clarity then you yourself will not be able to read your script, let alone understand it.

Firstly, there has to be a decision that resonates with: "*I will be an enlightened millionaire.*" Then, you have to state your intention and commit it in writing. Writing your statement brings more clarity to your thought process.

Lastly, you have to announce it to the whole world that you are going to be an enlightened millionaire by a particular date—tell your friends, family and the whole world about your intentions. It will put pressure on you; instead it will keep you focused. You have to burn your bridges behind you to succeed. Without commitment, there is no clarity.

Goals are very critical to your success. They have to be clearly defined and practically achievable. To keep yourself balanced, you can record different goals in major areas of your life like health, relationships, intellectual, spiritual and financial goals. You have to write them, read them, see them and talk about them in every waking or dreaming moment of your life. You will then see your goals magically materialize into your life.

To become an enlightened millionaire you have to make a decision, state your intention and set goals. You have to live from your goals and think about them day and night.

Clarity and focus in your script will accelerate your pace of growth like nothing else. Can you imagine writing an article without a topic or a heading? The article will be confusing to the readers – it will be unintelligible. Similarly, without stating your goal and intention, your life script will be full of confusion.

To gain clarity you have to state your goals and put them in writing. You have to view and repeat these goals on a daily basis to stay on track and in focus. It looks simply but you will be surprised to learn that over 99% of the population has no stated goals and as a result, drift along in life. To be successful, you have to state your goals clearly and stay focused.

Be Congruent

There is a difference between a goal and an agenda: you can have a clearly stated goal but your hidden agenda can often sabotage that goal.

Our hidden agenda is normally driven by our ego, deep seated prejudices and value systems. Our hidden agendas are like saboteurs who are out to destroy our most well laid plans. We have to find these little saboteurs and convert them to our side.

To succeed you have to be congruent. You have to align your mind, body and spirit to a single purpose. Ask any top athlete. At the crucial point of winning-losing, they have their mind and body dissolves into one. There is no thought but only singularity of purpose. This singularity of purpose makes them champions.

The greatest loss of energy takes place because of attrition in the mind. When there is conflict of goals with our value system the script gets corrupted. We have to turn deep within ourselves to understand our hidden prejudices and value systems. We have to either bring in change to our inner attitudes or modify our goals to bring them into alignment with our core values. Without this, we will be working at cross purposes that will be deterrent to our success.

By little observation you can find out if there is a conflict within your mind and belief system.

People who complain of lethargy usually suffer from some kind of an inner conflict. One way to resolve such a conflict is through understanding the flow of energy. When everything is in alignment, there will be no noise and friction in the mind. If you are congruent, there will be explosion of energy within your system. Your script will then have clarity and sense of its purpose.

Transformational Change

Here we are not talking about increments in your script – we are talking of how you can achieve a quantum jump that can transform you instantly. It is transformational learning as against informational learning that is predominant in our educational system that defines our script.

Informational learning is passive; teachers talk and students listen. It is about memorization, examinations and grades. Teachers talk about subjects on which they have theoretical knowledge, but lack practical experience—such an education can never be inspirational.

Transformational learning is about self-discovery. The student is given an inspirational stimulus by a mentor who has traveled the path and has discovered the answers to the problems through his experience.

All the knowledge to become a millionaire is already within you. No one can teach you how to become rich. Someone can only inspire you to awaken every cell in your body that will cry out that you were born to be rich and free, and to live a life of abundance. It is your natural state.

Transformation occurs when the right stimulus is given to awaken what is inside us and our script changes instantaneously.

Mentors

The shortcut to transformational knowledge is to find a mentor; they are invaluable! They have travelled the path and they have the knowledge. They will stir you in their presence. A word of advice from them will transform you. It will be a life changing experience that no book, DVD or tape can provide.

Where can you find Mentors?

The truth is you cannot find a mentor until you are ready. The day you are ready a mentor will appear. A little preparation is required at your end to receive a mentor.

No one can inspire you until you are ready to be inspired. No one can change you until you desire the change. No one can make you rich until you want to be rich. When this happens, a mentor will appear in your life and take you forward in leaps.

There are mentors all around us but we don't see them because we are not mentally prepared for them. We associate ourselves with losers, time wasters, frivolous and non-productive people. How can we eject magnetic waves to attract successful people?

To gain some magnetic power, we have to initially force ourselves to the presence of people who emanate powerful doses of the magnetic energy we want. Association is a very powerful thing. If you associate with the right kind of people, you will be subjected to the right kind of energy fields. This will transform you. You will also become a magnet attracting the right kind of people. There is nothing new in it – it is the basic law of attraction.

"The soul attracts that which it secretly harbors, that which it loves, and also that which it fears. It reaches the height of its cherished aspirations. It falls to the level of its chastened desires – and circumstances are the means by which the soul receives its own." As a Man Thinketh by James Allen (1864 - 1912)

A mentor carries a hundred times stronger energy field. He can transform us to a different level instantly. However, we will receive the energy only once we are mentally prepared to accept the energy.

Thoughts have an energy that attracts like energy. A mentor will come to us when we are ready and not a day before that. We have to develop our thoughts (conscious and unconscious,) emotions, beliefs and actions to a certain level in order to attract the positive energy from a mentor.

If you study the lives of wealth creators, you will find they have been mentored not by one but several mentors at different periods of their lives. A mentor will not only fill the gaps in your knowledge but will inspire you to new levels of achievement, which you think is not possible.

They will change your thought process and internal script.

Is it expensive to get mentors? Not necessarily. If you are serious and dedicated, you can get mentored for free. All masters take on assistants to do their 'grunt work,' so that they can leverage their time. You can volunteer to become their apprentice.

There is a Chinese proverb that goes like: "*A single conversation across the table with a wise man is worth a month's study of books.*" You can invite a mentor to a meal—it works like a charm.

The Millionaire Mind-set Scripts

We do not have to do anything spectacular to change our script to an 'enlightened millionaire's mindset,' but make small changes to alter the initial condition that can change the long-term trajectory of our lives.

T. Harv Eker in his brilliant book, Secrets of the Millionaire Mind, has written about wealth files or scripts for mastering the inner game of wealth. Some of the scripts are discussed in the succeeding paragraphs. These scripts are very powerful and can cause a 'Butterfly Effect.' You may apply some or all of them to change the outcome of your life. Please study these scripts carefully and start applying them gradually to your daily lives.

Rich people believe 'I create my life'. Poor people believe 'Life happens to me'

Enlightened millionaires take responsibility for their life and actions. They do not blame others when things go wrong. On the other hand, poor people think they are the victims and are experts at the 'blame game.' They blame the government, the economy, their bosses, friends and family when they fail. Blaming others for them is like a stress reducer. Complaining and justification are like pills they become addicted to.

You can either be rich or a victim—it depends on what script you choose. You slit your financial throat each and every time you choose to blame others. So choose to stay above the line. At the end of each day, carry out a complete debrief and write down each situation and how you handled it. This will dramatically change the outcome.

Rich people play the money game to win. Poor people play the money game not to lose

In sports, you can never win a game by playing defense; you have to be offensive and score if you have to win. I once saw a table tennis match—a really good player playing offence was matched against a defensive opponent and I had never seen a defensive player of his caliber. He was a virtual returning machine: he would stand twenty feet away from the table and continue returning the smashes from his opponent. It forced the smasher to make mistakes as he was the aggressor. The crowd cheered for the defensive player as he was unique or probably they identified with him. The aggressive player made several errors and lost points, but in the end, he won handsomely to the disappointment of the crowd.

I was in the Navy and in every war game we played offensive tactics to beat any purely defensive strategy. We also found that it was nearly ten times cheaper to build or buy an offensive weapon platform – like a missile boat or an aircraft launched missile – than to provide a credible defense against the threat.

The same holds true for the money game: truly rich people go on the offensive. Their goal is to acquire massive wealth. They shoot for the stars. Poor on the other hand, want to be comfortable. They never want to stick their necks out or pick up a challenge. They are always on the defensive, acting within their comfort zone. Security is of paramount concern to them. As a result, they never win and never get rich.

Rich people are committed to being rich. Poor people want to be rich

The number one reason most people don't get what they want is that they don't know what they want. Rich people are totally clear that they want wealth. They are unwavering in their mind and are fully committed to creating wealth. They will do whatever it takes, as long as it is moral, legal and ethical.

Based on the Laws of Attraction, the universe will conspire to help them achieve their goal because the message the rich send out to the universe is very clear – they want to be rich! The poor on the other hand, send out confused messages because of the negative wealth files. "What if I can make money and then lose it all? I'll be in the highest tax bracket and will have to give away half the money to the government—it's too much work. My health may suffer. I will have no time for my family. I'll never know if people like me for myself or my money...my kids could be kidnapped."

Most poor people want to be wealthy but have a confabulating script and a vague desire to be rich. This is why they do not succeed. The rich on the other hand have a script that is fully committed to creating wealth—devoid of any confusion whatsoever. They want to travel, have time on their hands, provide best possible things to their loved ones or help others and give money to charity. If you want to commit, then put your goals in writing and read them morning, evening and night. Announce your commitment to the entire world. Be congruent in thought, emotion and action. Clarity of purpose leads to success.

Rich people think big – Poor people think small

The difference between the rich and the poor is only a couple of zeros behind their incomes and net worth statements. It is as simple as that.

There is a saying: "Size of the question determines the size of the result." If you ask yourself a question: "Can I earn $30,000 doing this?" Then you will get the wrong result. If you ask yourself the question "How do I create or earn a million dollars?" Then your mind goes to work in a different direction. It wants to find a solution and works ceaselessly to find a satisfactory answer.

Most people fail to ask the big question – they choose to play small. They are frightened of failure and even scared to death of success. Our life is not about shrinking and feeling insecure—life is all about expansion and discovering our true worth. As we expand and liberate from our fears, our very presence liberates others from their small attitudes. Think big; there is no greatness in being small.

You will be a millionaire if you start thinking like a millionaire. Want to be a billionaire? Then learn to think big like a billionaire—it is all in the mind and beliefs you have.

Rich People focus on opportunities. Poor people focus on obstacles

Rich people see opportunities – poor people see obstacles. Rich people see potential growth – poor people see potential loss. Rich people focus on rewards – poor focus on risks. The mindset of the poor is, "It won't work." The mind-set of the rich is, "It will work because I will make it work."

What you focus on expands. If you focus on opportunities, they will expand. On the other hand, if you focus on obstacles, they will look insurmountable. If you want to be rich, focus on making, keeping and investing your money. If you want to be poor, focus on spending your money.

Rich people see an opportunity, jump on it and get richer. The poor look at the obstacles and keep preparing to overcome them. They never take action, which is why they lose.

Action always beats inaction. Rich people get started after understanding the risks; they make adjustments and corrections as they move along. If you want to be rich, focus on opportunities and take action.

Rich people admire other rich and successful people. Poor people resent rich and successful people

One of the surest ways to remaining poor is to resent the rich. Most poor people are conditioned to believe that one can't be both rich and spiritual simultaneously or be rich and a good person.

There can be nothing further from truth. To create wealth, certain human characteristics are needed. One has to be intelligent, hardworking, reliable, focused, determined, persistent and positive. Moreover, the person has to be a good communicator with a high degree of human skills and integrity. Without some of these skills coming into play, it is impossible to become rich in the first place.

There may be a few exceptions wherein people have become wealthy through ill-gotten means. However, in my experience such wealth never lasts for long. Seek inspiration from the enlightened rich who are, by far, some of the nicest people. They have reached where they are because of their expanded mental state and positive attitude to life.

Practice the Huna philosophy which states, *'**Bless that which you want'**.* Write a letter or an email to someone successful you admire. Tell them how much you admire and honor their achievement. You will develop an instant connection to success.

Rich people associate with positive, successful people. Poor people associate with negative or unsuccessful people

Easiest and fastest way to create wealth is through association. Be with the rich and learn how they became rich and mastered the game of money. 'If they can do it, I can do it'.

You must have heard the old adage: "Birds of a feather flock together." This is very true because most people earn within 20% of the average income of their closest friends. If you want to soar, fly with the eagles and don't get stuck swimming with the ducks.

Being in company of negatively minded people can be infectious. You can get measles of the mind.

Instead of itching, you get bitching and instead of irritation, you get frustration.

It is not your job to reform negative people. You must keep away from them. Once you develop the positive energy field around you, they will get influenced by it but not before that.

In the initial stages, you must charge your energy field by hanging around with winners. Read biographies of the extreme rich and successful: Warren Buffet, Bill gates, Steve Jobs, Donald Trump, Andrew Carnegie and the likes.

Join clubs which the rich frequent. Identify friends and family who pull you down and stay away from them. Stop watching trash television and stay away from bad news that could potentially pollute the mind. ***Rich people hang around with winners. Poor hang around with losers***. Never forget this basic principle.

Rich people are willing to promote themselves and their value. Poor people think negatively about selling and promotion

People who have issues with selling are usually broke – it's obvious. How can you create a large income in your business, or as a representative of one, if you aren't willing to let people know that you, your product, or your service exists? Even as an employee, if you are not willing to promote your virtues, someone who is willing will bypass you on the corporate ladder.

Poor have the fear of failure and rejection. They feel it is impolite to blow one's own trumpets. The world has so many products and services that nobody has the time for you or your product if you are not willing to step up and project yourself.

The poor have an attitude that makes them naively believe in their uniqueness. Hence, promotion is beneath them. Poor believe that because they are so special, someone will find them ultimately. They remain broke because of this attitude.

You may have the best talent and the product but no one will know of it if you are unwilling to promote. This is because everyone in the world has an information clutter and no time for you. You have to rise above the clutter and make yourself be heard.

Rich people are always excellent promoters. They know how to package their ideas, products and skills and they promote them with enthusiasm and passion. Robert Kiyosaki, author of the best-selling 'Rich Dad Poor Dad' series of books calls himself the "best-selling" and not the best writing author.

Every business depends on selling. Money is made only when something is sold in the market place. To become rich, you have to learn the art of promoting with 100 percent integrity. This can be done through courses in marketing and sales or reading books on the subject. People who shy away from this vital aspect cannot hope to amass wealth.

Rich people are bigger than their problems. Poor people are smaller than their problem

Poor people want to run away from problems – they don't want hassles and headaches. They will sweep them under the carpet or close their eyes like ostriches to wish them away. Problems have a habit of rebounding with a great vengeance. The more you try and avoid them...the poorer, broke and miserable they will keep you.

The secret to success is not to try to avoid or get rid of or shrink from your problems; the secret is to grow yourself so that you grow bigger than the problem.

The rich are problem solvers. They make money by identifying a problem and find a solution for it. People will pay money to solve their problems.

If by training you become level-10 problem solvers, do you think a level-5 problem will cause any worry or stress to you? The secret is to grow bigger than the problem.

The first step is to write down all the problems you are having in your life and then list actions to resolve them—this simple exercise will make your growth process to become bigger than your problems.

Your income will directly relate to the level of problem you are willing to solve. If you are an employee, you are solving a problem for your boss. You will get fired once you become a problem for the organization. If you are in business, you are solving problems for your clients. Be it servicing a car, providing plumbing services or pulling out a tooth. The quality of service and level of problem you are willing to solve will determine success of your business.

Rich people are excellent receivers. Poor people are poor receivers

For every giver there has to be a receiver, and for every receiver there must be a giver. One of the reasons why poor remain as poor is because they are poor receivers. They may or may not be good at giving but most certainly, they are poor receivers.

This holds true in every walk of life. To be loved, we have to know how to receive love. The universe has infinite abundance of wealth—it has to go somewhere. There are trillions of dollars floating around. If we are not ready to receive our share, it will go to someone who is willing to receive.

Being open to receiving is absolutely critical to creating wealth. There are times when money flows into our lives, we should accept the blessing of the universe gracefully and accept it as a gift. Once you learn the art of receiving, you will become a money magnet and start attracting money.

Rich people choose to get paid on results. Poor people choose to get paid based on time

The thumb rule to becoming rich is: "***Never have a ceiling on your income***." *Poor people trade time for money. The problem with this strategy is that your time is limited. This means that you are breaking the fundamental rule of becoming rich which means having no ceiling on your potential income.*

Rich people prefer to get paid in results. If they run a business, they get paid from the profits. Alternately, they prefer to work on profit sharing, stock options or commissions.

In the financial world, rewards are proportional to the risk one is willing to take. What the poor do not realize is that job security comes at a price and that price is wealth. You can make a small start by requesting your employer to pay you partly based on the results. Another option is for you to set-up your own small business or consulting company, or to join a network marketing company and become result oriented.

Rich people think "both." Poor people think "either/or."

Rich people live in a world of abundance and poor people live in a world of limitations. Both live in the same physical world, but the difference is in their perspectives. Poor people think that either I can be rich or be spiritual.

Rich people think they can be both. Poor people think that either they can spend time with their families or work hard to become rich. Rich people think they can balance both.

Rich people believe "***You can have your cake and eat it too***." The middle-class people believe "***Cake*** *is too rich, so I'll only have a small piece*." The script of the rich is to be creative and find ways for having "both."

The rich focus on their net worth; the poor on their working income

The vocabulary of the poor consists of: "How much I earn" or "How much I make." The rich, on the other hand, think of their net worth' and "How much profit I made." *The true measure of wealth is net worth, not working income.*

The words that write your script define your future. If you think in terms of 'earning' as opposed to 'net worth,' you will stay put in your job of trading time for money. *Where attention goes, energy flows and results show*. So, focus your attention on the right script to increase your income. Simplify your life style to reduce your cost of living and invest the savings or surplus amount. Create a net worth statement and revise this statement every quarter to help analyze your progression.

Rich people manage their money well, Poor mismanage their money well

Rich people are good at managing their money though they are not necessarily smarter than the poor; they just have a different approach towards money.

This small difference in habit makes the biggest difference in the financial outcome of being rich or poor. Poor people either mismanage or they avoid the subject of money altogether. The excuse generally given is either, "It restricts our freedom" or "We don't have enough money or time to manage."

Nothing can be further from truth, because managing money allows financial freedom. ***The habit of managing your money is more important than the amount.*** Until you learn how to handle what you've got, you are most likely not to get any more.

Rich people have their money work hard for them. Poor people work hard for their money

Most of us are programmed "***to work hard for money.***" The rich on the other hand, reprogram themselves "**to make their money work hard for them.**"

Working hard has never made anyone rich—working smart is the way to riches. The more your money works, the less you will need to work.

The definition of financial freedom is the ability to live the lifestyle you desire without having to work or rely on anyone else money. Therefore, to become free you will need to earn money without working. To do this you will need to create a passive income wherein money keeps flowing in whether you work or not.

The sources of passive income working for you can be either financial instruments like stocks, bonds, mutual funds or businesses working for you that are in confluence with: real estate, royalties from books, music or software, licensing your ideas, network marketing etc.

These will be discussed in depth later in the book. In simple terms: poor people work hard and spend all their money, which results in them having to work hard forever. Rich, on the other hand, work hard, save and then invest their money so they never have to work hard again.

The key is to change the money blueprint from immediate gratification to thinking long-term. Balance your spending on enjoyment today with investing in freedom tomorrow.

You will need to change your "Material gratification" files and replace them with "Financial freedom" files. Change your focus from "Active income" to "Passive income." List out strategies you can put to work to generate passive income.

Rich people act in spite of fear. Poor people let fear stop them

Fear freezes us to act and our well laid plans fail to manifest; thoughts lead to feelings, feelings lead to actions and actions lead to results.

We may have all the right knowledge but unless we act, there can be no wealth creation. ***Action is a bridge between the inner and the outer world***. Rich and successful people have fear; they have doubts and worries like the rest of us but they do not allow these fears to stop them.

Poor people on the other hand, allow their fears to limit them. To change our scripts, we have to break the habit and make a conscious effort to act in spite of doubt, in spite of worry, in spite of uncertainty and discomfort. We have to learn to act even if we are not in a mood to do so.

Rich people constantly learn and grow whereas poor people think they already know.

*The three most dangerous words in English are "**I know that**." So how do you know if you know something? It is simple. If you live it, you know it. Otherwise, you heard about it, you read about it, or*

you talked about it, but you do not know about it.
To know about it, you have to live it. If you are not
really happy, there's a good chance you still have to
learn about money, success and life.

Poor people generally try and prove that they are right and they have got it figured out; it is just a stroke of bad luck or a temporary glitch that has them broke and struggling.

There is an excellent saying by Jim Rohn that makes perfect sense here: ***"If you keep doing what you've always done, you'll keep getting what you've always got".*** If you are unsuccessful and not willing to change your life script or take the trouble to educate yourself, then you will keep getting the same results again and again. Someone rightly said, ***"Definition of madness is to keep doing the same thing again and again and expect a different result."***

There is a constant need to learn and grow; everything alive is constantly changing. If a plant is not growing, it is dying. It is true for every organism including human beings. If you are not growing, then you are dying.

Author and philosopher, Eric Hoffer, has rightly said, ***"Learners shall inherit the world while the learned will be beautifully equipped to live in a***

world that no longer exists. " This means that if you are not constantly learning and growing you will be left behind.

Poor people usually complain that they do not have either the time or the money to get educated—these are plain excuses. The only thing normally lacking is the commitment to learn and change. Rich people, on the other hand, relate to Benjamin Franklin's famous quote: "***If you think education is expensive, try ignorance.***"

Poor people seek advice from relative and friends who are equally clueless. This keeps them entangled in the web of poverty. The most expensive advice you can ever receive is free advice from an ignorant person.

Rich, on the other hand, continuously read books and attend seminars to improve the skills and strategies they need to accelerate their income, manage their money and then invest it effectively. They learn the game of money from those who are the masters in the field and have success become a corollary of it.

Your income is directly related to your inner growth, which includes: financial, emotional and spiritual IQ. You must commit to your growth and consider hiring personal coaches to keep you focused and on track in the various aspects of your life, including health.

The outer world is merely a manifestation of your inner world. There are outer laws of money that entail: business knowledge, money management and investment strategies.

Equally important are the inner laws, or the script that defines you as a person. It is not enough to be at the right place at the right time. You have to be the right person in the right place at the right time.

Fear, which is the biggest enemy of wealth creation, can – to a large extent – be controlled by expanding our financial, emotional and spiritual intelligence. The internal change in the script is critical before we can learn about the outer laws of wealth creation which in comparison are very easy to master. Once the internal transformation is complete, there is no force on earth that can stop you from becoming a millionaire.

Driving Force behind Wealth Creation

What drives you to create wealth is a very important factor that will determine your success. Deeper your motivation, stronger will be your foundation to create wealth.

If your desire to create wealth is motivated by external factors – such as buying a luxury car, going on a holiday, or moving into a larger house – then they are not formidable enough to take you very far. There is nothing wrong with these desires, but they can be satisfied soon enough. Money can buy you things, but not happiness.

Similarly, if acquiring wealth is motivated by greed or fear then it will not bring you happiness. These motivations are non-supportive and therefore, not deep enough to create sustained wealth.

To create long-term wealth, you have to be driven by an inner drive that is hard to satisfy. These may include: search for freedom from a job you do not like, to pursue your passion, your hobbies and sports. One of the great internal motivations can be the pursuit of personal growth including health.

The strongest innate motivation is the desire to help others—elevate them from their sufferings or teach them, using your own example as muse, how to create enlightening wealth. By pursuing a deeper cause, you will not only bring about transformational change within yourself but also the ones around you.

There are always challenges in creating wealth. It is easier to overcome those challenges once you motivation level is deeper than superficial.

Certain actions and changes in your everyday life may act as stimulus to understanding your deeper motivation. Firstly, give more value than you take from others: when you give value to others, you improve your own life. Wealth created by exploiting others never lasts long, and does it provide any internal happiness.

There should be a high level of integrity in your everyday actions. You cannot cheat your way into any meaningful wealth. Your mind is a great powerhouse; keep it pure and creative. Don't waste your energy in the pursuit of wealth through shortcuts and by causing harm to others.

The deeper and nobler your cause, greater will be your wealth. Such wealth will also provide you with inner happiness and peace.

Final Thoughts

Inner transformation always precedes wealth creation. I failed in my first few attempts at business not because of lack of hard work or effort, but because I was not adequately mentally prepared for business. My wealth grew in proportion to the inner change that was taking place within me.

Awareness of the inner principles of wealth creation is one small step and transformation will not happen overnight; combing action and experience will speed up that process. Constant education, associating with the right groups of people, and deep reflection will play a huge role if you wish to progress on the path of acquiring a wealthy mindset. Try and seek mentors at each stage of your growth—it will hasten your growth process. Make small changes in your life and observe the butterfly effect play out.

Whether you are an employee, self-employed, an investor or in business—applying the principles enunciated this book will help you grow financially. Slowly but surely you will embrace abundance which is your birth right.

The purpose of this book will be served if it helps in educating and help morph enlightened people who create wealth the right way, preserve wealth the right way and ultimately, use their wealth for the greater good of humanity. This process leads to seeking a higher purpose in life and its fulfillment. I hope and pray that to some extent, that purpose is served. If you have read to this point, I thank you with gratitude in my heart and hope you succeed in creating true wealth that helps not only you and your family but entire humanity.

If you liked the book and gained some knowledge that will be useful to you in life, then please leave an honest review to help others find this book. It will be a small effort on your part, but an act of charity that may help in changing few lives for the better. I thank you in advance for your help.

This book is about fundamental principles of wealth creation that can be applied to any business or investing strategy. At Wealth Creation Academy, we teach multitude ways to generate passive income, which includes: real estate investing, digital publishing, affiliate marketing, multi-level marketing and investing in forex, commodities, and shares by copying experienced traders that need very little of time. You may like to get started with some of the strategies depending on your budget and time.

Other Books by the Author

Praveen Kumar has authored several bestselling books. Please visit his website http://praveenkumarauthor.com/ for more information

About the Authors

Praveen Kumar was abandoned by his father at the age of fourteen and joined the Navy at tender age of fifteen where education, roof and free food were guaranteed.

In order to understand the root cause of suffering he turned towards philosophy and religion. After 10 years of soul searching and meditation he understood that 'life is 'and material and spiritual world are closely interwoven. You cannot live in one without the other.

Praveen was highly successful in the Navy, where he successfully commanded submarines, sailed around the world in a yacht and received gallantry award for his contribution to the Navy.

Despite his success in the Navy, Praveen realized that lack of financial security for his family was one of key root causes of his suffering, resulting from his childhood deprivation. To improve his financial standing, Praveen took pre-mature retirement from the Navy to build his financial future through investing in Real Estate. The decision to educate on financial matters paid off, and today he and his wife are comfortably retired on six-figure passive income.

His aim is to help others create wealth in an enlightened way and empower them to live a healthy and happy life. He dedicates his time to write books and articles on financial and spiritual matters.

Prashant graduated with distinction from Auckland University as a computer engineer and later completed his MBA from the world's leading institution - INSEAD. During his successful corporate career, he worked for the most reputable consulting firms in the world - BCG & Deloitte - and represented New Zealand on Prime

Minister-led trade missions to South East Asian countries.

After successfully generating income through his passive investments in property and stocks, Prashant decided to team up with his father to help people transform their lives through the leverage of financial education.

Their website http://wealth-creation-academy.com/ is devoted to teaching people how to create Multiple Streams of Passive Income through investing in real estate, online marketing and creating digital products